happiness is ...

happiness is ...

200 ways to be creative

Lisa Swerling & Ralph Lazar

CHRONICLE BOOKS

SAN FRANCISCO

a different viewpoint

being handy with tools

Z Y X W V U T S...

doing things your own way

fancy handwriting

working together

finding new ways to express
your ideas

free-flowing thoughts

embracing your style

accepting
impermanence

marching to your
own beat

tall tales

a group of like-minded friends

decorative flair

turning off your
computer

a quiet place

blogging

doing things the old-fashioned way

comic improv

There was a young man from Bengal...

being silly

seeing life as art

a complicated scavenger hunt

investing in your talent

an out-of-season picnic

the first page of a blank book

being the best at something

getting some perspective

turning heads

documenting real life

cultural immersion

teaching someone
a new skill

a new obsession

jotting down ideas

cooking by taste

perfecting
a routine

finding beauty in the everyday

a thorough reorganization

letting it all
hang out

playing with
your materials

using what you have

getting your
groove on

pure originality

unapologetic positivity

finishing what you started

watching a movie on mute and
recreating the dialogue

inventing a silly walk

dreaming of
the future

improvising

having confidence in your opinions

focusing on technique

learning from other cultures

concentrating
on the details

making something to share

a successful
partnership

being your
own person

slowing down

enthusiastic amateurs

teamwork

getting started

working with your hands

a restorative catnap

reliving the good old days

enjoying your own company

busting out

being immersed
in the moment

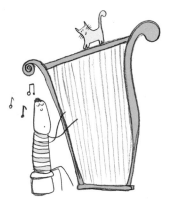

doing something you've
been putting off

the pursuit of
excellence

getting your hands dirty

new experiences

fixing up rather than
throwing out

knowing you
look fabulous

making the most of the weather

alone time

recharging
your batteries

making something
from scratch

starting over

building something out of boxes

a special card

burning the midnight oil

a new collection

playing with scale

ignoring the rules

the perfect solution

recording a great idea before you
forget it

listening

taking ten deep breaths

an ambitious project

being brave

working hard

writing yourself
a love letter

popular culture

dancing along to your own tune

surrounding yourself with smart,
open-minded people

being asymmetric

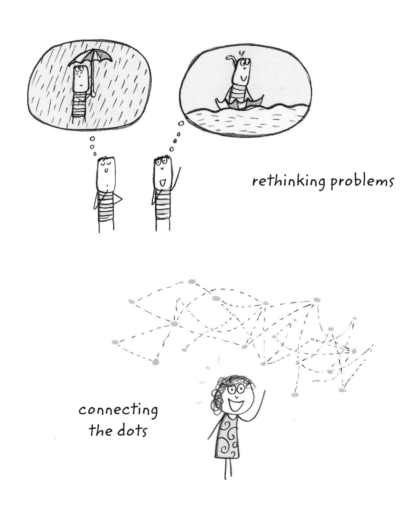

rethinking problems

connecting
the dots

taking your goals seriously

crafting with friends

a change of environment

contagious positive
energy

homemade party accessories

making
time to dream

taking a
well-deserved break

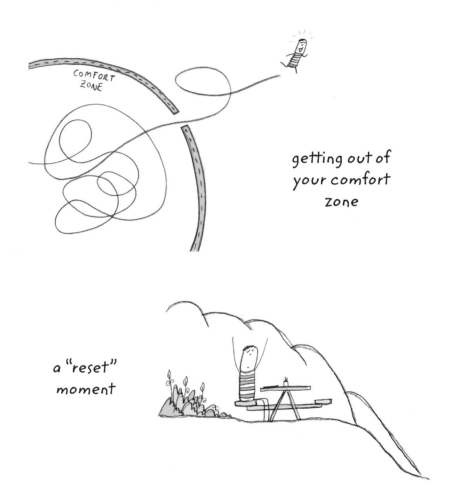

COMFORT ZONE

getting out of your comfort zone

a "reset" moment

brainstorming

ignoring practicality

a unique point of view

being open to new ideas

enjoying the
unexpected

not taking yourself
too seriously

a well-told story

taking a class

curiosity

creating space

thinking big

following a stranger's
advice

letting your mind wander

experimenting

re-purposing

close observation

becoming a
beginner again

seeing the world through
new lenses

a new configuration

accepting change

mixing, not matching

more than the
sum of its parts

trying anything
once

creating a beautiful environment

learning
a new trick

imaginary conversations

letting kids
lead the way

a new style

contributing to
a good cause

smushing all the
colors together

creating something new from
something old

embracing every
moment

clearing your head

getting carried away

when inspiration strikes

turning your wardrobe
into a work of art

taking the lead

working with distractions

living by your own rules

getting messy

decluttering

risk-taking

an inspiring partner

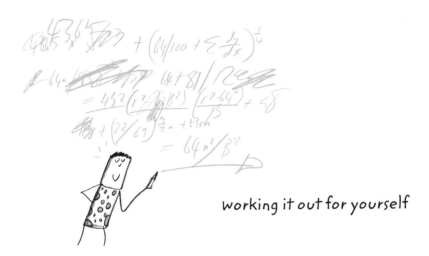

working it out for yourself

a natural talent

planning
something epic

taking inspiration
from nature

unplugging

taking the road less traveled

turning dreams into reality

a travel journal

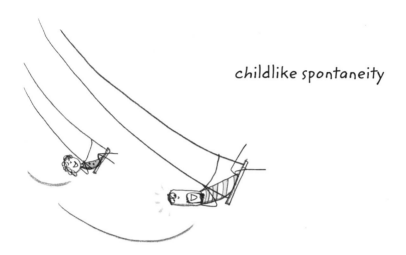

childlike spontaneity

making something in
your downtime

learning from the greats

brand new
art materials

doing a small job well

doodling

going off the beaten track

seeing life as exploration

thinking out of the box

being awesome

drawing in the margins

practicing till it's perfect

channeling your inner child

internet inspiration

taking an idea to its limit

self-expression

remembering that
anything is possible

persistence rewarded

sweet collaboration

simplifying

noticing small details

ditching your ego

taking every project seriously

a reading
marathon

a homemade garment

balancing risk
and reward

stream of
consciousness

new hobbies

diving deep into
your thoughts

making something just for fun

long-term plans

a clean space

a leap of faith

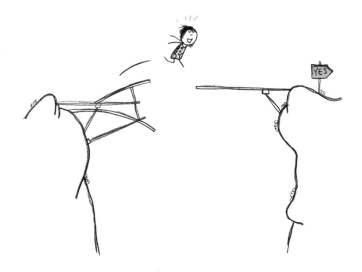

abstract
expression

the perfect muse

getting back
to basics

laughing at yourself

domestic pizzazz

engaging with
politics

a blank canvas

an innovative solution

bouncing ideas
off people

public recognition

doing what you love

ISBN 978-1-4521-4629-4

Manufactured in China.

Design by Lisa Swerling and Ralph Lazar

10 9 8 7 6 5 4 3 2 1

Chronicle Books LLC
680 Second Street
San Francisco, California 94107
www.chroniclebooks.com